Soliloquy: A Compilation of Inner Thoughts

Oakbee Powers

BookLeaf Publishing

Soliloquy: A Compilation of Inner Thoughts
© 2023 Oakbee Powers

Presentation by *BookLeaf Publishing*

Web: www.bookleafpub.com

E-mail: info@bookleafpub.com

ISBN: 9789358368987

First edition 2023

DEDICATION

To my grandmother, Velvet, whom I loved and will continue to love with all of my heart. Life will never be the same without you.

ACKNOWLEDGEMENT

I would like to thank my biggest supporters in life, and the ones who encouraged me to join the contest that resulted in the publication of this compilation.

To my sister, Chelsea, thank you for always encouraging me to get outside of my comfort zone.

To my mom, thank you for providing me with the confidence to publish these poems.

To my stepdad, thank you for teaching me to work hard for what I want.

To my former teachers— Mrs. Kirby, Mrs. Dotson, and Mrs. Flagle— thank you for feeding my passions in school.

To my former coaches, Mrs. Trimble and Mrs. Calloway, thank you for being there for me and teaching me that I am important, no matter how I perform.

To my friends— Will, Kelsi, Atlas, Toby, Gabby, and everyone else— thank you for giving me objective and useful feedback on my work. I appreciate it more than you know.

And, last but not least, to my therapist (who I'm sure would prefer not to be named for legal reasons), thank you for working with me for all these years. This book wouldn't be possible if I hadn't met you.

To those I didn't explicitly mention by name, thank you all as well. All of you helped build a support system for me at a time when I needed you.

To all, regardless of mention, I love you. And one last time, thank you.

Queer

Queer.
Strange,
Weird,
Unclean.

Queer.
Different,
Dangerous,
Diseased.

But then, there's the change.
Society grows and contorts into different shapes.

So, queer.
Beautiful,
Complex,
Natural.

Queer.
Soft.
Loving.
Carefree.

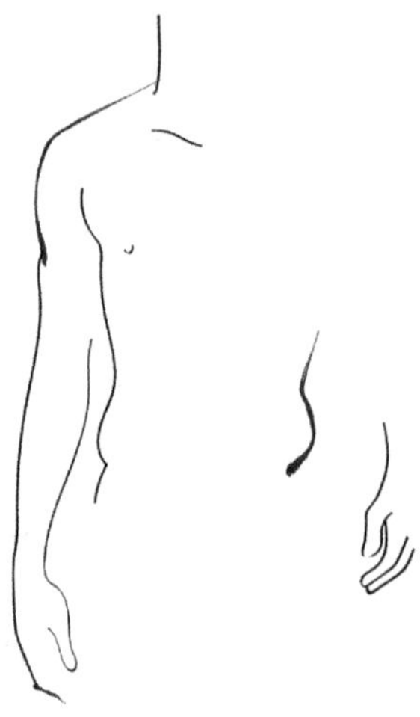

Curriculum

Consume, consume, consume.
What's appropriate for a child your age?
Who knows?

You can't learn about menstrual cycles.
God, no.
But you can learn about the development of
weapons throughout World War II.
Forget the fascism. That's not too important.

The state says that teachers can't discuss their
partners in school.
Of course, that's only true for those who don't
conform to their expectations.

Claiming to make education more accessible,
But continuously putting teachers in situations
where they feel manipulated and pressured to
teach the bare minimum
In order to keep their jobs.

Separation of church and state
Is rolling in its grave.

Judge

Yes, sir.
No, sir.
Could I please be frank, sir?
I feel like the world is crumbling all around me,
sir.
Like soon I'll be thrown into chaos all by
myself, sir.

College is approaching, sir.
I'll be away from my family and pets, sir.
I'm quite uneasy, sir.

The government is becoming increasingly more
powerful, sir.
I live in a world in which I cannot make
decisions about my own body, sir.
I live in a world in which I cannot fly any flags
that I identify with for fear of harm, sir.

I'm tired, sir.
I am.
I humbly ask you for your consideration on this
matter, sir.
If you don't mind, I'd like to travel through
time, sir.

Forward to when all of my problems are solved, sir.
To when everything is in balance, sir.
To when I can truly be me without fear, sir.

I humbly request a decision on this matter, sir.
Please.

The Girl Who Cried Wolf

The boy who cried wolf was quite lucky in the
end.
If he were the girl that cried wolf,
He never would have been believed at all.

The girl that cried wolf knew that he was
dangerous.
But when she called for help, no one came.

"I know the wolf," her mother said. "I grew up
with him. He would never do such a thing."

"Are you certain?" her father asked. "This could
ruin his career, you know."

The townspeople whispered around, saying
things like "it must be her fault! She should have
been more modest!"

The girl that cried wolf was a victim,
But all of the blame in the world clouded her
neighbors' minds.

And when they found her at the top of the hill,
Shivering in the cold and wet,
She was all alone.
She would never be the same.

Ballad of the Brain

The beating of your heart sounds within your
head,
The heavy breaths your lungs are taking in
weigh heavy on your scrambled mind.
Your brain brandishes your worries against you
like a weapon.

A weapon of your mind's own making,
Bladed and coated in titanium,
Razor sharp.

Near neuropathy of neurons.

Move On

I don't know what I'm doing.
I've been set on this same path for years now,
My inquisitive nature demanding that I acquire
knowledge every day.
I always thirst for more.

But somehow, I always end up the same.
My work scattered around me in the form of
notes, botched efforts, and abandoned projects.
And so I move on,
Because if I am not perfect the first time,
I never will be.

I search and I search and I search for something
to satisfy me.
Something that I may be a prodigy in.
But someone will always best me,
And so I move on again.

My records are repeatedly soiled by those who
are better suited than I.
Anything other than a win is a devastating loss.

Passing exams with flying colors until I don't.
I'll never be good enough for my own good.
So I move on, and I become someone else.
All over again.

Words Carry Weight

Words carry weight.
We mull them over,
Turning them in our mouths and
Rolling them on our tongues like
Sisyphus, pushing his boulder for all of eternity.

Poets are our Hades,
Forcing us to pour our energy
Into our speech every time we
Open our cavernous mouths
And spill our thoughts like a
Toddler dribbles juice down their chin.

But we can mold the terrain
Around our rock, and level those
Humongous hills of dread and
Negativity built up around us.

We are not too small
To make a difference.
We can lift that tonnage.
Even ants can carry up to
5,000 times their own mass.

Cicatrix

I want to be unique.

I want to grow old with callouses and scars.
I want to point at my body and be able to tell
stories.

Like "that's the time I accidentally hurt my hand
while cooking."

Or "my fingers have those rough spots because
of how long I played the oboe."

Or whatever else comes to pass in life.

Maybe I'll get surgery on my back to fix my
spine's curvature.

Maybe I'll have double incisions across my
chest and say "that's from when I put myself
first."

Maybe I'll have to explain that my writing
callous is on my right index finger because of
the way I hold my pencils.

But no matter what, I'll just be glad to be
myself.
To have my own experiences in life.
To have my own cicatrices.

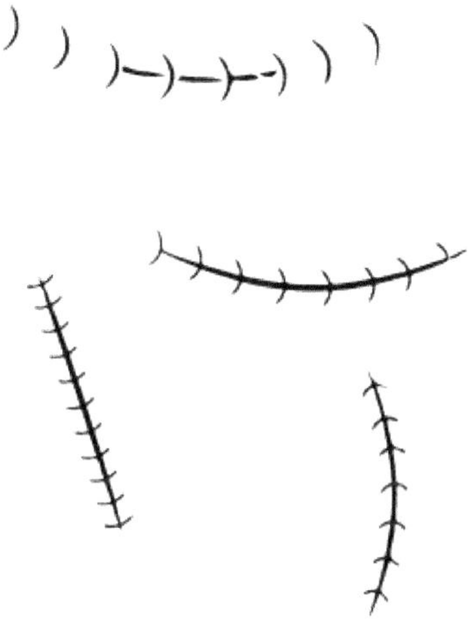

Dog

Dog,
Loose from his leash and collar.
Where will he go?

Maybe he'll find a nice tree to sleep under over
the hill.
Maybe he will chase his tail in circles until he
loses sight of it.
Maybe he is chasing a new toy,
One that his owner bought him--
A ball? Or a bone?
Maybe he is running just to run,
Just for fun.

Ah, that's it!
That girl over there,
She threw a stick!
There he comes,
Trotting back with it in his mouth,
Running quick!

Go Away

There's nothing worse than waking up in the
morning,
Having that momentary bit of bliss
Before you forget that they're gone.

When you wake up and you think
"I should go check in on them."
And then it settles in, like a ghoul perched on
top of your chest.

When you feel like you just need to go back to
sleep,
To chase that moment.
But you know that you can't, and instead you
just sit up in bed,
Trying to rid yourself of the painful thoughts
running through your head.

But they won't go away.

"Boys Will Be Boys"

"Boys will be boys"
Applies to situations where boys
Play,
Laugh,
and Spread joy.

"Boys will be boys"
Does not apply to situations where boys
Bully,
Harass,
and Assault.

Boys celebrate joy and embrace kindness.
That's just who they are.
Until they are conditioned to do otherwise.

Boys warn against anger and condemn violence.
That's just who they are.
Until they are conditioned to do otherwise.

Extraterrestrial

22

A crater in the earth,
A sign of deep impact in the sand,
A sort of vehicle left behind.

A set of footprints,
A slimy trail,
A single specimen cowering in a seaside cave.

A loud laboratory,
A bright light,
A multitude of sharp instruments.

A mutilated creature,
A frightened and defenseless animal,
A defenseless extraterrestrial.

Alphabet Soup

He's four years old.
He knows his ABCs.
He stirs his spoon around in his soup.

"Daddy," he says.
"What does this mean?"

"L-O-V-E?" his father says.

"Yes, that word," the boy answers.

"Love is…" his father begins.
But how do you explain such an abstract concept
to a child?
The words swirl around in his mind.
"Love is… like Mommy and I. We love each
other very much."

"Why?" the boy asks.

"We just do. Just like I love you."

"I'm glad," he says.
He starts to stir his spoon around again.
"And… what does this mean?"

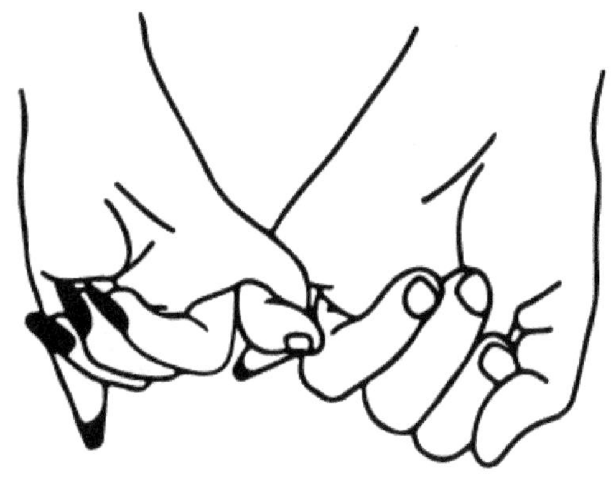

Mask

25

Hide,
Trick,
Run,
Sneak,
Crawl.

Put your mask on and pull it tight.

Disguise,
Deceive,
Break,
Mend,
Assimilate.

Keep your mask on and draw it tighter.

Dodge,
Weave,
Sit,
Speak,
Listen.

Keep your mask on and tighten it until it and
your face are one.

Arrive at home,
Sit in bed,
Put your headphones on,
Draw up the covers,
Lay against your pillows.

Take the mask off. You can be you.

Places to Be

Rolling around in fresh sheets,
My hair fluffing against the pillows at my
headboard,
I smile to myself.

There are a lot of places that make me feel nice.
I like water, and I like museums,
But my bed is definitely my top choice when it
comes to places to be.

My dog jumps up next to me,
Barking his little head off.
I smile to myself.

There are a lot of places that make me feel nice.
I like aquariums, and I like zoos,
But my room is definitely my top choice when it
comes to places to be.

I open my window,
The wind swelling in cools me.
I smile to myself.

There are a lot of places that make me feel nice.
I like labs, and I like libraries,

But my home is definitely my top choice when it comes to places to be.

28

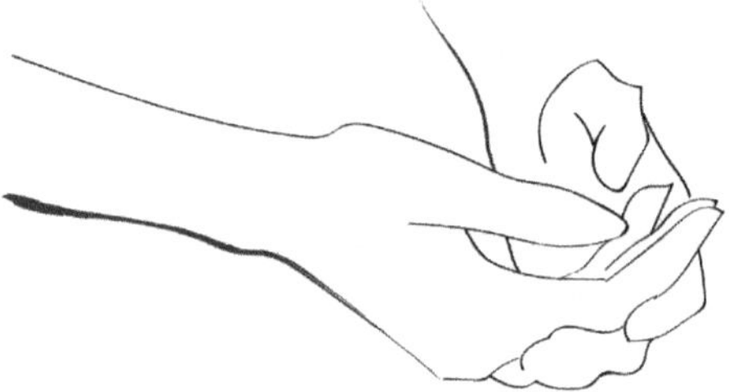

Mobile

The moon and the stars swirl above my head.
I sit back in my comfortable place and observe.
They look especially bright tonight, don't you
think?

I can't help being comforted by the fact that no
matter how far away they are,
The heavens are in my line of sight.
I feel as if I could reach up and touch the
satellites above.

I stand up, my soft domain fading away.
But I can barely feel it.
I want to hold the moon in my hands.

I bet it would be warm.
The yellow light reflecting off of its surface
would feel amazing.
I'd bask in it.

My hand grazes the surface.
I'm so close!
But I fall down, back into the springy mattress
below me.

It was cold.
The moon was cold.
And so were the stars.

Schadenfreude

We cry.
They smile.

We beg.
They laugh.

We suffer.
They delight.

We ask for our rights.
They deny.

They campaign.
We smile.

They tour.
We laugh.

They lose approval.
We delight.

They ask for votes.
We deny.

Et Tu, Brute?

In the sunlight, a blade glimmers.
He brings it down into his victim.
It tears through his muscle.
Terrified, he utters that phrase.

"Et tu, Brute?"

The breath catches in his attacker's throat.
He looks down into his victim's eyes.
They look for his humanity with desperation.
It is nowhere to be seen.

"Sic semper evello mortem tyrannis."

The weapon is drawn from his side and plunged
back into his heart.
All is silent in the murderer's ears.
His comrades cheer at the fall of the man's
corrupted regime.
But he remains silent.

Drunken with power, and weighed with guilt, he
finally stands.
He tries not to show emotion, but his eyes
continue to grow wet.

"Sic semper evello mortem tyrannis," he whispers.

"Sic semper tyrannis."

The Importance of Science

Every day I wake up and I think that, as scientists,
We've discovered it all.
Of course, I'm always wrong.
But that's what's so great about science.

I love waking up to things that amaze me.
Sometimes I think
"How did we get so far without this?"
That's the usual.

I love reading the news.
"Scientists continue cancer research."
"5,000 new deep sea animals found in Pacific Ocean."
"Home built partly by recycled diapers."

I love finding hope in the new,
So that I can ignore the cruel old world.
I love thinking about what's to come,
So that I can put the past behind me.

So, here are my thoughts.

I think that humanity is so conditioned to the old,
That it's enamored with the new.

I think that humanity lives in the now,
But yearns for the future.

I think that we all have hopes for a bigger and better world,
But that we lose ourselves in them, instead of pushing for that place.

And I think that we, as a group, come closer every day.

To me, that's the importance of science.

Click Here!

Click here!
Buy this machine!
It can tell you with absolute certainty
Whether your husband is lying,
Or if your mom is hiding things from you.

Click here!
Buy this miracle cream!
It can heal you with absolute certainty
Whether your skin is dehydrating,
Or if you're dying from an incurable disease.

Click here!
Buy this magazine!
It can tell you with absolute certainty
Whether your favorite actor is marrying,
Or if your favorite musician is singing the blues.

Click here!
Buy this clothing!
It can tell you with absolute certainty
Whether your size is increasing,
Or if your waist is shrinking rapidly after that
new fad diet.

Mamaw

Sometimes when I talk about my family, I'm
embarrassed.
Not because I don't love them,
Or because I'm ashamed of them,
But because of the way I talk.

When I don't think about it, I say the funniest
things.
I call my grandmother my Mamaw, and my
mother my Mama.
I always get strange looks from those that don't.

It's even worse when I'm out of town,
Or out of state.
That's when I get the most comments.

"Wow, you sound so different!" people say.
What they really mean, of course,
Is that to them, I seem uneducated, because of
my syntax.

But people are more than how they sound,
Or where they're from.
They're what they love, and who they love.
They're defining moments, and experiences.

Anyway, I'm tired of watching how I speak,
Or of deliberately changing my choice of words.
I should be able to show affection however I
want.

I'm not ashamed of being from Appalachia.
It's beautiful, and rife with culture.
Communities are tight, and love is central to our
ways of life.
And I love my Mamaw, as well as my Mama.